VOCAL SELECTIONS

Where's Charley?

BY FRANK LOESSER

Applications for performance of this work,
whether legitimate, stock, amateur, or foreign, should be addressed to:
MUSIC THEATRE INTERNATIONAL
545 8th Avenue
New York, NY 10018
(212) 868-6668

ISBN 0-7935-4290-1

FRANK MUSIC CORP.

EXCLUSIVELY DISTRIBUTED BY

HAL•LEONARD® CORPORATION

7777 W. BLUEMOUND RD. P.O. BOX 13819 MILWAUKEE, WI 53213

VOCAL SELECTIONS

BY FRANK LOESSER

CONTENTS

THE STORY OF THE SHOW

A MUSICAL OF THE VICTORIAN ERA, PRESENTING A MOST AMUSING STUDY OF THE SOCIAL MANNERS OF THAT PERIOD. IT IS GRADUATION WEEK AT OXFORD AND CHARLEY AND HIS ROOMMATE, JACK, HAVE INVITED THEIR LADY FRIENDS, AMY AND KITTY, TO LUNCH IN THEIR ROOMS. THIS IS A DARING GESTURE, BUT SINCE CHARLEY'S AUNT, DONNA LUCIA (A VERY RICH WIDOW FROM BRAZIL), IS ARRIVING TO VISIT CHARLEY, SHE CAN CHAPERONE THE FOURSOME—SO AMY AND KITTY AGREE TO THE PLAN.

DONNA LUCIA DOESN'T ARRIVE AS SCHEDULED AND WHEN THE GIRLS ARRIVE THEY FIND CHARLEY COSTUMED AS AN ELDERLY WOMAN—HE IS REHEARSING HIS PART FOR THE SCHOOL PLAY. FOR FEAR OF NOT HAVING THE GIRLS' COMPANY FOR LUNCH, JACK INTRODUCES CHARLEY AS DONNA LUCIA AND FROM THEN ON HE IS IN CONSTANT CONFLICT—PORTRAYING BOTH HIS AUNT AND HIMSELF.

MY DARLING, MY DARLING

By FRANK LOESSER

LOVELIER THAN EVER

By FRANK LOESSER

THE NEW ASHMOLEAN MARCHING SOCIETY AND STUDENTS CONSERVATORY BAND

By FRANK LOESSER

WHERE'S CHARLEY?

By FRANK LOESSER

PERNAMBUCO

By FRANK LOESSER

ONCE IN LOVE WITH AMY

By FRANK LOESSER

Slow and easy soft shoe

Verse

I caught you, sir, hav-ing a look at her As she went stroll-ing by. ___ Now, did-n't your heart beat boom, boom, boom, boom, boom And did-n't you sigh a sigh? I warn you, sir, don't start to dream of her. Just bid such thoughts be - gone ___ Or it - 'll be boom, boom,

boom, boom, boom, boom, boom, Boom, boom, boom, boom ___ from then on, For

Chorus

ONCE IN LOVE WITH A - MY, ___ Al-ways in love with A - my. ___

Ev - er and ev - er fas-cin-at-ed by 'er, Sets your heart a-fire ___ to stay.

Once you're kissed by A - my, ___ Tear up your list, it's A - my. ___

Ply her with bon-bons, po-et-ry and flow-ers, Moon a mil-lion hours a - way. ___ You

MAKE A MIRACLE

By FRANK LOESSER